Happily Ever Crafter

ONCE UPON A
ROBOTS
AND ALIENS
CRAFT

ANNALEES LIM

Lerner Publications ◆ Minneapolis

First American edition published in 2020 by Lerner Publishing Group, Inc.

First published in Great Britain in 2018 by Wayland
Copyright © Hodder and Stoughton, 2018
All rights reserved.

Senior Commissioning Editor: Melanie Palmer
Design: Square and Circus
Illustrations: Supriya Sahai

Additional illustrations: Freepik

Lerner Publications Company
A division of Lerner Publishing Group, Inc.
241 First Avenue North
Minneapolis, MN 55401 USA

For reading levels and more information, look up this title at www.lernerbooks.com.

Main body text set in Billy Infant Regular 17/24.
Typeface provided by SparkyType.

Library of Congress Cataloging-in-Publication Data

Names: Lim, Annalees, author. | Sahai, Supriya, 1977– illustrator.
Title: Once upon a robots and aliens craft / Annalees Lim, Supriya Sahai.
Description: Minneapolis : Lerner Publications, [2019] | Series: Happily ever crafter | Audience: Age 7–11. | Audience: Grade 4 to 6. | "First published in Great Britain in 2018 by Wayland."
Identifiers: LCCN 2018050609 (print) | LCCN 2018053626 (ebook) | ISBN 9781541561984 (eb pdf) | ISBN 9781541558809 (lb : alk. paper)
Subjects: LCSH: Handicraft—Juvenile literature. | Robots in art—Juvenile literature. | Aliens in art—Juvenile literature.
Classification: LCC TT160 (ebook) | LCC TT160 .L48526 2019 (print) | DDC 745.5—dc23

LC record available at https://lccn.loc.gov/2018050609

Manufactured in the United States of America
1-46269-46261-11/27/2018

SAFETY INFORMATION:
Please ask an adult for help with any activities that could be tricky or involve cooking or handling glass. Ask adult permission when appropriate.

CONTENTS

sci-fi WORLDS

For now, a world filled with robots and aliens only exists in our imaginations. But people often think about the future and all the new technologies that have not been invented yet. Future worlds that we see in science fiction stories could become a reality soon!

Extraterrestrial is a long word, but it simply means "not from Earth." Alien life can be the smallest bacteria or microbes that live on meteors or planets. Often, we think of aliens as little green men with large eyes zooming through our atmosphere in flying saucers. While there is still no evidence for the existence of aliens, it does not stop human beings from trying to find proof. There are many programs all around the world dedicated to learning more about the universe we live in.

FACT!

UFO stands for unidentified flying object. It is used to describe things that fly in the sky but are not birds, aircraft, or anything from Earth. Some people think they are alien spaceships, but this has never been proven.

Robots are real! Robots are any machine programmed by a computer that can do things with little or no human contact. We have been using robots for years. They do jobs that humans find hard or boring to do. They help make our cars, explore the deep oceans, and even get sent into space.

You can have lots of fun making up your own sci-fi world. Will yours be filled with giant metal robots that are operated by small, squishy aliens? Or perhaps you will create your own spaceship that you can fly to explore new solar systems. The only limit is your imagination, and this book, filled with craft ideas, games, and lots more, is a great place to start. You can become the ultimate space and time traveler using the out-of-this-world things you have created!

TOP TIP
Collect things like old newspaper and plastic containers from around the house for your craft supplies. They can be used for the fantastic projects you will find in this book.

OUTER SPACE OUTFITS

Transform yourself into crazy cosmic characters that are perfect for any party. These fantastic ideas are easy to make by yourself but are fun to make with your friends too. You can make these projects really unique by using spare materials you have lying around your home.

ROBOT

Robots were built to help humans do jobs that we find difficult. They are very useful to have around because they don't get tired and never need to stop for food or drink. How helpful can you be when you dress up in your own robot costume?

You Will Need:

- LOTS OF CARDBOARD BOXES
- TIN FOIL • GLUE STICK
- SCISSORS • 2 STRAWS
- SCRAP PAPER • BOTTLE LIDS
- TAPE • SILVER DUCT TAPE

1. Make a cardboard headband that is at least 6 inches tall from a flattened box. Cover it in tin foil.

2. Decorate this with scrap paper to make the robot's face. The eyes and mouth shouldn't have round edges.

3. Make some antenna for your headband from two straws and more scrap paper.

4. Lay out lots of flattened cardboard to make a torso—remember to include a hole for your head. Stick together with silver duct tape.

5. Decorate the torso with small cardboard circles covered in foil. Add colorful bottle lids for buttons and dials.

ALIEN

Aliens come in all shapes and sizes, from little green men to scary sharp-toothed monsters. You can create your own sci-fi style and come up with an alien design that is as unique as you are. Sketch your ideas first and use this project as your starting point.

You Will Need:

- LARGE CEREAL BOX
- SCISSORS • CARDSTOCK
- GREEN PAINT • PAINTBRUSH
- WHITE CRAFT GLUE • GREEN TISSUE
- PAPER OR MAGAZINE PAGES

1. Cut off the top of the large cereal box and cut a "U" shape from the front. Make sure it is large enough for you to see out of.

2. Cut out some large eyes on stalks and some antenna from scrap cardstock.

3. Stick these onto the top and sides of the box using craft glue.

4. Paint the whole thing using different shades of green and leave to dry.

What's an alien's favorite drink?
Gravi-tea!

5. Add strips of green tissue paper or magazine pages to the bottom of the box to look like alien tentacles.

STAR TIARA

Stars are made up of burning balls of gas. They glow brightly, and we can see them at night. Scientists use color categories to tell them apart. There are red, yellow, and even blue stars. Make your tiara full of colorful stars to match the universe.

You Will Need:

- CARDBOARD OR OLD HEADBAND
- TIN FOIL • TAPE • LARGE PLASTIC BOTTLE • SCISSORS
- SCRAP PAPER • THREAD

1. Make a cardboard headband or recycle an old headband. Cover it in tin foil.

2. Ask an adult to cut up a plastic bottle into five rings. Cover the edges with tape so they're not sharp and wrap in foil.

3. Use a stapler to attach the rings to the top of the headband.

4. Cut out two identical star shapes that are no bigger than the plastic rings. Cut a slit on the top of one and the bottom of the other.

5. Slide them together and tape some thread to the middle. Attach to the ring so it spins inside. Repeat to make more stars for the rest of the rings.

DID YOU KNOW?

Our sun is actually a star that is billions of years old. Even though it looks big to us, it is one of the smaller stars in the galaxy. Other stars look smaller in the night sky because they are farther away.

ASTRONAUT JET PACK

There is no gravity in space, and it can be hard to go in the direction you want when you are floating around. Jet packs (or propulsion units) help astronauts move in space when they are outside the spaceship. Make yours and see how fast it makes you zoom!

You Will Need:
- 2 LARGE PLASTIC BOTTLES
- NEWSPAPER • WHITE CRAFT GLUE
- TAPE • PAINT • PAINTBRUSH
- PLASTIC BAGS • SCISSORS • RIBBON

1. Remove the lids from the two bottles and tape them together side by side.

2. Use craft glue to cover the bottles in torn-up pieces of newspaper, then leave to dry.

3. Paint the bottles white with red stripes and leave to dry.

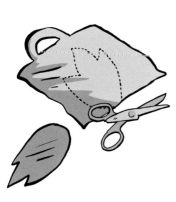

4. Make flames from old colorful plastic bags and stuff them inside the bottle necks. Hold in place with tape.

5. Make some straps so you can wear your jet pack by taping on long pieces of ribbon.

PLANET PARTY

If you're planning on celebrating a special occasion with an outer space theme, have a look at our helpful hints. Follow these steps to help you stay organized and remember the most important things you need to make your party a success.

5, 4, 3, 2, 1 . . . BLAST OFF!

The countdown has begun to the launch of your party, and there is a lot to get done! Look at this list of things to help you organize and prepare for the event.

5 . . . SPACE! Party themes are a great starting point to help you turn any dull space into a whole new world. You could choose to create your own space station, an alien planet, or even a futuristic version of your house with cool new inventions and gadgets. Find some inspiration with the decoration ideas on page 16.

4 . . . A GALAXY OF GAMES! Discover fun new games to play on page 12. You can give out prizes to the winner of each game or keep a scoreboard to see who has won the most games and gets to be crowned the Leader of The Universe!

3 . . . ROCKET FUEL! Your guests will need lots of energy to keep up with all the space adventures you have planned. Use the recipes on page 20 for ideas on what to serve.

2 . . . GOODY BAGS! Say thanks to your guests by giving them a small gift. Look at the craft ideas on page 24 and see what things you can make them.

1 . . . SPACE MISSION! Make it your mission to have as much fun as possible. You've done lots of planning and made lots of cool things, so remember to enjoy yourself and have a blast!

INTERGALACTIC INVITES

You have a fantastically futuristic theme, but who will you invite? Look at this great rocket invitation template. You could use it to invite your best pals and include all the information they need.

To Space Cadet:

To Space Cadet:
Add your friend's name.

The Countdown has begun to the Launch:
Add the date and time of the party.

The countdown has begun to the launch on . . .

Come to the Space Station:

Come to the Space Station:
Add the address of the party.

RSVP:

RSVP:
Ask people to let you know if they can make it.

PARTY GAMES

These simple party games will be a big hit at your party. Easy to make and fun to play, they will keep your guests entertained for hours. Make a spaceship scoreboard to keep track of the winners of each game.

COGS AND GEARS

Cogs and gears are wheels that have teeth. They fit together in machines to make things go faster or slower or have more or less power. They fit together in different combinations of shapes and sizes to make a gear train.

You Will Need:

- MAGAZINE PICTURES
- SCRAP CARDBOARD • TAPE
- BLACK MARKER • SCISSORS
- GLUE STICK

1. Stick a magazine page picture onto a piece of scrap cardboard.

2. Use the tape roll as a template to draw five circles onto the back of the cardboard.

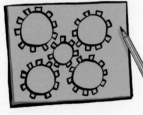

3. Draw square "teeth" around each circle so that the cogs fit into one another.

4. Cut these out carefully and keep them together in a pile.

5. Repeat this to make a set of cogs for each player. Make sure you choose a different picture for each player.

HOW TO PLAY

Each player hides another player's set of cogs around the house. Everyone meets back in one place for the countdown. After counting down from ten, each player goes off to find their set of cogs. When they have found them all, they go back to the meeting place and race to put their cogs in the right order and make the picture. The fastest player wins.

SPACESHIP DISC GOLF

Humans have been traveling to space for years, but we have never traveled farther than the moon. There is an International Space Station where astronauts can live and do research. It stays in one place and orbits Earth, which it does more than fifteen times a day. Space programs are working to find ways humans can travel farther into our solar system.

You Will Need:
- 2 PAPER PLATES PER PERSON
- STAPLER • SCISSORS • PENCIL
- MARKERS OR PAINT
- CONSTRUCTION PAPER

1. Cut out a circle in the middle of your paper plate. Use this as a template to draw and cut out a circle in the other paper plate.

2. Staple them together to make the spaceship.

3. Decorate with paint or markers.

4. Fold five bits of paper in half to look like cards. Decorate each with a number between 1 and 5.

HOW TO PLAY

Place the card numbers around an outside space. Stand in one spot and throw your disc toward the number 1. If you have not reached it, throw again from where it landed. Count how many throws it takes you to get to the number 1. Stand at the number 1 and throw to the number 2. Count again to see how many throws it takes you. The winner is the person who completes the course in the fewest throws.

2

1

5

4

LASER BEAM OBSTACLE COURSE

Lasers are very powerful beams of light made using mirrors and atoms. We use lasers in lots of machines, to cut things up, and even to play DVDs.

1. Fill the small bottles with a handful of rice. Screw on the lid.

2. Decorate the bottles by gluing on strips of paper.

3. Cut out lightning bolts from yellow paper and glue them onto the bottles.

You Will Need:
- 3 PLASTIC BOTTLES WITH LIDS
- RICE • CONSTRUCTION PAPER
- SCISSORS • GLUE • RIBBON OR STRING

HOW TO PLAY

Wind the ribbon or string around things to make an obstacle course. If you're playing outside you can wrap around trees, and if you're inside you can wrap around chairs or other sturdy pieces of furniture. Balance the bottles on top of the laser beam strings in different locations. Start the timer and carefully walk through the beams to try and collect the bottles. If you bump into too many laser beams at once a bottle might fall and you will lose. The winner is the person who collects the most bottles in the least amount of time.

MIGHTY METEORS

You Will Need:
- LARGE PIECE OF CARDBOARD
- PAINT • PAINTBRUSH
- SMALL PEBBLES

Most meteors are small bits of rock that have broken off of a comet. As they fall from space toward the earth they usually burn up and look like shooting stars in the night sky. Any that reach planet Earth without burning up completely are called meteorites—but you'd be lucky to find one!

1. Paint a large piece of cardboard black. A flattened out cardboard box is perfect.

2. Paint white circles onto the black and add some large and small stars inside each circle.

3. Write 10, 20, or 30 on each star.

HOW TO PLAY

Place the board on the ground and have everyone else stand about ten steps away. Take turns to carefully throw the meteor rocks onto the board. Once all the rocks are thrown, count up the points. 0 points for landing off the board, 10 points for landing in the 10 zone, 20 points for landing in the 20 zone, 30 points for landing in the 30 zone, and negative 10 points for every meteor rock thrown into the black hole in the middle.

4. Paint five pebbles in the same color. Make a set for each player.

PARTY DECORATIONS

Decorating your party space doesn't need to cost lots of money to make a big impact. Try these easy crafts that are inspired by undiscovered, faraway worlds filled with robots and aliens.

SOLAR SYSTEM HANGINGS

A solar system is made up of planets, moons, asteroids, and other things that orbit a star. The star sits in the middle and everything else rotates around it in a large oval called an ellipse. Our solar system has eight planets that are all different in size and appearance.

1. Cut construction paper into strips of the same length. You will need about twenty strips total.

You Will Need:
- CONSTRUCTION PAPER • HOLE PUNCH • SCISSORS • STRING

2. Punch a hole at both ends of each strip.

3. Stack the strips on top of each other and thread a piece of string through one end. Tie a big knot so that the string does not fall through the hole.

4. Fan the strips around in a circle and bend each one into an arch before threading it onto the string.

5. Tie another knot at the top to fix the strips into a globe shape.

16

FLYING ROCKET SHIPS

Sputnik 1 was the first spacecraft to be launched into space in 1957. Since then, many shuttles, spacecraft, and probes have been sent to space with unusual names like *Luna, SpaceX Dragon,* and *Helios.* Make your very own and add it to the collection. Remember to give it a name.

1. Make four tubes by cutting two paper towel tubes in half.

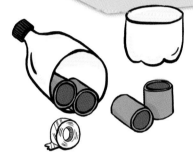

2. Cut off the top of a plastic bottle and tape the four tubes inside the hole.

You Will Need:
- 2 PAPER TOWEL TUBES • LARGE PLASTIC BOTTLE • CARDSTOCK
- SCISSORS • BLACK MARKER
- WHITE CRAFT GLUE • TAPE
- NEWSPAPER • PAINT • PAINTBRUSH

3. Draw four fin shapes from some cardstock. Cut them out and tape them to the bottle.

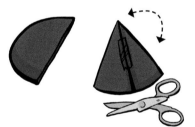

4. Cut half a circle from some cardstock and roll it into a cone. Stick to the top of the bottle.

TOP TIP
Hang the ship up from the ceiling to look like it is zooming through space.

5. Cover the whole thing in a layer of torn-up newspaper and glue. Let it dry before painting it.

17

GIANT ROBOT

This robot can be made as big or small as you want. Use lots of small boxes or one giant one to change the look of your robot. You can also cut some holes out of the front of the boxes to hide things inside for your guests or use it as a display for all your birthday presents.

You Will Need:
- LARGE BOX • MEDIUM-SIZED BOX
- 4 SMALL BOXES • 2 YOGURT CONTAINERS
- TIN FOIL • WRAPPING PAPER • SCISSORS
- WHITE CRAFT GLUE • COLORED MARKERS

1. Cover the largest box in old wrapping paper. If you use the opposite side of the paper, it will be an off-white color that you can draw on.

2. Glue some yogurt containers onto either side and draw on the face.

3. Take the medium-sized box and cut out the front. Cover this with more wrapping paper.

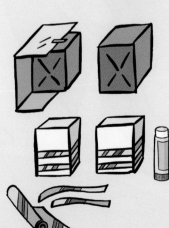

4. Cover the four smaller boxes in wrapping paper and add strips of tin foil as decoration.

5. Stick all your boxes together using craft glue and let dry before standing up.

MILK CARTON
MARTIAN

The word *Martian* means an alien from the planet Mars. Mars is one of the closest planets to Earth. You can see the planet from Earth without a telescope, so keep a lookout for what looks like a large red star on a really clear night.

You Will Need:
- PLASTIC MILK CARTON • SCISSORS
- WHITE CRAFT GLUE • GREEN PAINT
- GREEN AND BLACK MARKERS

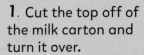

1. Cut the top off of the milk carton and turn it over.

2. Mix together some white craft glue and some green paint.

3. Paint the carton and leave it to dry.

4. Use a permanent marker to draw on some large alien eyes and slits for a nose.

5. Use a dark green marker to add other decorations to the alien head.

TOP TIP
Use a battery-powered LED tea light inside the Martian head to make it glow and give an eerie alien feel to your party.

SPACE FOOD

Serve up these spectacular space treats for your guests to enjoy. Display your fabulous food on a table decorated with all the things you have made. Food labels are a great idea too, so everyone knows what they are eating (see page 27).

COMPUTER CONSOLE CAKE

The first computer game ever made was a tennis-style arcade game called *Pong*, released by Atari in 1972. Since then computer games have become increasingly popular and moved from arcades to virtual reality games in people's homes.

You Will Need:

- SQUARE SPONGE CAKE
- KNIFE • DISPLAY BOARD
- FROSTING • BLACK FOOD COLORING
- CANDY MELTS • ICING PENS
- BLACK LICORICE

1. Mix together the frosting and a few drops of black food coloring.

2. Cut the sponge into one large rectangle and two smaller ones. Place them onto a display board. Cover the sponge in a layer of frosting and press some candy melts into the wet frosting to look like buttons. Let it set.

3. Cut up some lengths of licorice and join the large rectangle to the smaller rectangles.

4. Use an icing pen to add decorations to the cake. You can add more buttons, lights, and a logo.

LASER BLASTER
GELATIN

This sonic space shooter is straight out of the films of the 1940s, known as the golden age of science fiction. These films grew in popularity as people became interested in the space race, a competition where countries were racing to be the first to travel into space.

1. Cut the plastic bottle in half and place on a baking tray. You may need to roll up some newspaper and set it on the outside of each half so they don't tip over.

You Will Need:
- RED LICORICE LACES • FLAVORED GELATIN • BAKING TRAY • TAPE
- PLASTIC BOTTLE • SCISSORS
- KNIFE • LARGE PLATE
- (OPTIONAL: NEWSPAPER)

2. Fill the two halves of the bottle with gelatin and leave to set.

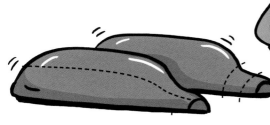

3. Tip out the gelatin and cut into sections.

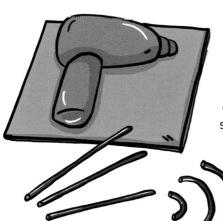

4. Reassemble the pieces on a large plate to make the shape of a laser blaster.

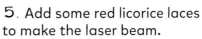

5. Add some red licorice laces to make the laser beam.

BLACK HOLE CHOCOLATE PUDDING

A black hole is sometimes made when a star dies. It has so much gravity that it pulls lots of things into it—even light, which is why you can't see it. A really big black hole is called a supermassive black hole. Black holes can only be found using special equipment.

You Will Need:

- CHOCOLATE PUFF CEREAL • BAR OF DARK CHOCOLATE • BAR OF MILK CHOCOLATE • CLING WRAP • SPOON
- 6 SMALL BOWLS • WHISK
- PACKAGE OF CREAM CHEESE
- 2 TBSP POWDERED SUGAR
- SMALL CAN OF CONDENSED MILK

1. Slightly crush chocolate puff cereal with the back of a spoon. Add melted dark chocolate and mix well.

2. Line six bowls with cling wrap and spoon some of the chocolate mixture in.

3. Press the mixture into the sides so that you make a cup shape. Leave in the fridge until they are set.

4. Whisk the cream cheese, powdered sugar, condensed milk, and melted milk chocolate together and pour into the cereal cups. Leave to set in the fridge.

5. Tip out onto plates and remove the bowl and the cling wrap before serving.

OATY ALIEN EGGS

This alien egg recipe is a perfect sweet treat that is also healthy for you. It will give you lots of energy, so it is a really great way to refuel after a busy day of space exploration.

Do robots have brothers?
No, just transistors!

You Will Need:
- COCONUT FLAKES • 4 TBSP OATS
- 2 TBSP HONEY • 1 TBSP RAISINS
- 1 TBSP DRIED BLUEBERRIES OR CRANBERRIES • 1 TSP VANILLA EXTRACT

1. Add the oats, honey, raisins, berries, and vanilla extract in a bowl and mix well.

30 MINUTES!

2. Put in the fridge for about 30 minutes.

3. Split the mixture into ten equal parts and roll into egg shapes.

4. Roll each egg in some coconut and place on a tray.

5. Keep in the fridge until you are ready to serve.

COSMIC CRAFTS

Gather together all your space junk and transform it into fun gifts, decorations, or even prizes for the games you have been playing.

ALIEN ABDUCTION

Who will you choose to beam into your spaceship? Use a photo of someone you know and trap them in the beam of light to create this 3-D photo frame.

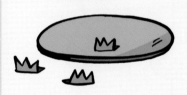

You Will Need:
- 2 PAPER BOWLS • CARDBOARD
- GLUE STICK • SCRAP PAPER
- SCISSORS • PLASTIC CUP
- PHOTOGRAPH

1. Cover a cardboard base in green paper. Add paper tufts of grass too.

2. Use a glue stick to sandwich together two paper bowls.

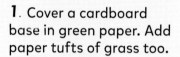

3. Decorate the bowls with scrap paper to create the spaceship.

4. Stick the plastic cup onto the bottom of the spaceship.

5. Cut out the photograph and place it inside the cup. Place the spaceship onto the grass.

LITTLE GREEN MEN

This slime can be molded, squished, and squashed into any shape you like. Add some googly eyes to what you make to create an army of slimy aliens.

1. Mix the craft glue and baking soda into a bowl with 1 cup of water.

2. Add a few drops of green food coloring and mix.

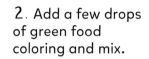

You Will Need:

- 1 CUP OF WHITE CRAFT GLUE
- 1 TSP BAKING SODA
- 1/2 CUP SHAVING CREAM
- 1 TBSP CONTACT LENS SOLUTION
- GREEN FOOD COLORING • GLITTER
- WATER • BOWL • GOOGLY EYES

3. Pour in the contact lens solution and mix until it turns into slime. You may need to add more solution to get it just right.

4. Take the mixture out of the bowl and knead well. Add the shaving cream to make it fluffier.

5. Add the glitter before you start to shape it into little aliens.

ROBOT PETS

Choose your favorite animal to turn into a robot. This project is to make a puppy, but you can use any animal you like to create your perfect pet!

You Will Need:
- 2 SMALL CARDBOARD BOXES
- TIN FOIL • WHITE CRAFT GLUE
- PAPER TOWEL TUBE
- SCISSORS • SCRAP PAPER

2. Cut up the paper towel tube into four equal pieces and cover with tin foil.

1. Cover the two small boxes in tin foil like you are wrapping some presents.

3. Stick the four tubes onto the bottom of one of the boxes and stick the other box on top of that.

WOOF!

4. Mold more tin foil to make a tail and an antenna. Glue them onto the front and back of the boxes.

5. Cut out bits of scrap paper to decorate the body. Make eyes, a nose, ears, and robot buttons.

SHOOTING STAR POP-UP CARDS

Use this simple pop-up craft to make party invitations, food labels, or even a thank-you card for the people who came to your party.

You Will Need:
- 2 PIECES OF CONSTRUCTION PAPER
- SCISSORS • GLUE STICK • MARKERS

1. Cut out two pieces of construction paper, one slightly smaller than the other.

2. Fold the smaller paper in half.

3. Cut five lines into the folded side of the paper.

4. Bend the cut section and open up.

5. Press the cut section in on itself and then glue it onto the large piece of paper.

27

ROCKET PORTHOLE

You Will Need:
- PENCIL • CONSTRUCTION PAPER
- SCISSORS • PAPER PLATE
- SILVER PAINT • PAINTBRUSH
- GLUE STICK

The International Space Station has an observational module called Cupola that has seven windows, giving magnificent views of space. But most spaceships are built without any windows at all because they make the ship weaker.

1. Use a pencil to draw around the paper plate onto a black piece of construction paper. Cut the circle out.

2. Carefully cut out the middle of the plate, leaving the edge intact.

3. Cut out small circles from the leftover black paper and stick around the plate edge.

What did the alien wear to his job interview?

A space suit!

5. Cut out stars and planets from construction paper and stick to the black paper. Glue the silver rim onto the outer edge.

4. Paint the paper plate silver and leave to dry.

SPACEMAN SALT PAINTING

The atmosphere in space is very different from Earth's, so it is important to protect astronauts when they travel. A spacesuit is important because it pumps in oxygen to breathe and is thick enough to keep the body from freezing in the cold temperature. It is also flexible so that the astronauts can move easily.

You Will Need:
- BLACK CARDSTOCK • WHITE CRAFT GLUE • SALT • PAINT
- WATER • PAINTBRUSH • PENCIL

1. Draw a picture of an astronaut onto the black card.

2. Trace over this picture by squeezing glue directly out of the bottle.

3. Sprinkle salt over the glue and gently shake off any extra.

4. Water down some paint and make sure your paintbrush has soaked up lots of the mixture.

5. Gently dab the paintbrush onto different areas of the picture and watch the paint spread. Repeat with other colors and see how they mix when they meet.

PLANET PRINTING

Did you know that until recently Pluto was considered the ninth planet in our solar system? It is now just called a dwarf planet. Scientists are still looking for planet number nine in our solar system, which they think could be ten times bigger than Earth. Can you predict what it will look like?

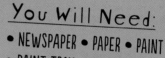

You Will Need:
- NEWSPAPER • PAPER • PAINT
- PAINT TRAY • CARDBOARD TUBE
- PAINTBRUSH • SCISSORS
- BLACK CONSTRUCTION PAPER
- COTTON SWAB • GLUE STICK

1. Scrunch up sheets of newspaper.

2. Evenly spread some paint onto the paint tray using a paintbrush.

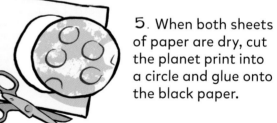

5. When both sheets of paper are dry, cut the planet print into a circle and glue onto the black paper.

3. Use the scrunched-up newspaper and cardboard tube to print paint onto the plain piece of paper. Use different colors of paint to make your planet unique.

4. Print small stars onto the black construction paper using the cotton swab and white paint.

SPACE EXPLORERS

Make a team of space explorers to travel the universe. Decorate each one of these models with different colors and designs to create aliens, astronauts, and robots.

1. Half fill the yogurt drink container with the small stones or rice.

2. Use the tape to fix the ping pong ball onto the top of the container.

You Will Need:
- SMALL YOGURT DRINK CONTAINER
- PING PONG BALL • SMALL STONES OR RICE • TISSUE PAPER • TAPE
- WHITE CRAFT GLUE • PAINTBRUSH
- PAINT • BLACK MARKER

3. Water down some craft glue and use this mixture to stick torn bits of tissue paper to the whole container.

4. Once it is dry, decorate your character using different colors of paint.

5. Add any details such as eyes or other features using the black marker.

SPACE PUZZLE

CAN YOU FIND THE ANSWERS TO THESE QUESTIONS?

1. How many stars can you find?

2. Which spaceship driver is different?

3. Who has the most eyes?

4. Which spaceship has the most fins?

ANSWERS: 1. 17 2. D 3. C 4. B

32